THE
POETICAL WORKS

OF

HENRY SCOTT RIDDELL

EDITED WITH A MEMOIR

By JAMES BRYDON, M.D.

HAWICK

IN TWO VOLUMES

VOL. I.

GLASGOW

MAURICE OGLE AND CO.

MDCCCLXXI

TO

THE MEMBERS OF THE

Edinburgh Border Counties Association

THESE VOLUMES

ARE RESPECTFULLY DEDICATED

IN ACCORDANCE WITH WHAT IS BELIEVED WOULD

HAVE BEEN THE COURSE TAKEN BY

THE AUTHOR.

CONTENTS OF VOL. I.

MEMOIR.

In placing before the world a narrative of the principal events in the life of Henry Scott Riddell, we are glad to be able to do so largely in his own words. It may seem strange that one so modest and unpretentious should have written an autobiography, but it was done to oblige a friend; and such was his nature that he would have put himself to any amount of trouble, or made any sacrifice, to accomplish this. In its present form, it is abridged from Dr Roger's 'Modern Scottish Minstrel,' for which it was originally written. He was born on the 23d Sept. 1798, at Sorbie, near Langholm, where his father, Robert Riddell, was a shepherd. His mother's maiden name was Agnes Scott, and both she and her husband were natives of Teviotdale. "My father, while I was yet a child," so runs the autobiography, "left Sorbie; but when I had become able to traverse both *burn* and *brae*, hill and glen, I frequently

returned to, and spent many weeks together in the
vale of my nativity.   We had gone, under the same
employer, to what pastoral phraseology terms ' *an
out-bye herding*,' in the wilds of Eskdalemuir, called
Langshawburn.   Here we continued for a number
of years, and had, in this remote but most friendly
and hospitable district, many visitors, ranging from
Sir Pulteney Malcolm down to Jock Grey, whom
Sir Walter Scott, through one of his strange
mistakes, called David Gellatly.   Among others
who constituted a part of the company of these days,
was one whom I have good reason to remember—
the Ettrick Shepherd.   Nor can I forbear observing
that his seemed one of those hearts that do not become older in proportion as the head grows grey.
Cheerful as the splendour of heaven, he carried the
feelings, and, it may be said, the simplicity and
pursuits, of youth into his maturer years ; and if few
of the sons of men naturally possessed such generous
influence in promoting, so likewise few enjoyed so
much pleasure in participating in, the expedients of
recreation, and the harmless glee of those who meet
under the rural roof—the shepherd's *bien* and happy
home.   This was about the time when Hogg began
to write, or at least to publish ; as I can remember
from the circumstance of my being able to repeat
the most part of the pieces in his first publication
by hearing them read by others before I could read

them myself. It may, perhaps, be worth while to state that at these meetings the sons of farmers, and even of lairds, did not disdain to make their appearance, and mingle delightedly with the lads that wore the crook and plaid. Where pride does not come to chill nor foppery to deform homely and open-hearted kindness, yet where native modesty and self-respect induce propriety of conduct, society possesses its own attractions, and can subsist on its own resources.

" At these happy meetings I treasured up a goodly store of old Border ballads, as well as modern songs: for in those years of unencumbered and careless existence, I could, on hearing a song, or even a ballad, sung twice, have fixed it on my mind word for word. My father, with his family, leaving Langshawburn, went to Capplefoot, on the Water of Milk, and there for one year occupied a farm belonging to Thomas Beattie, Esq. of Muckledale, who, when my father was in Ewes, had been his friend. My employment here was, along with a younger brother, to tend the cows. In the winter season we entered the Corrie school, but had only attended a short time when we both took fever, and our attendance was not resumed. At Langshawburn, my father for several winters hired a person into his house, who taught his family and that of a neighbouring shepherd. In consequence of our distance

from any place of regular education, I had also been
boarded at several schools—at Davington in Esk-
dale, Roberton and Newmill; at each of which,
however, I only remained a short time, making, I
suppose, such progress as do other boys who love
the football better than the spelling-book.

"At the Whitsunday term my father relinquished
his farm, and returned to his former employment in
the Forest of Ettrick, under Mr Scott of Deloraine,
to whom he had been a shepherd in his younger
days.   With his family, indeed, and that of Mr
Borthwick, then of Sorbie, and late of Hopesrigg,
all his years since he could wear the plaid were
passed, with the exception of the one just mentioned.
It was at Deloraine that I commenced the shepherd's
life in good earnest.   Through the friendly partiality
of our employer, I was made principal shepherd at
an age considerably younger than it is usual for
most others to be intrusted with so extensive a
hirsel * as was committed to my care.   I had by
this time, however, served what might be regarded
as a regular apprenticeship to the employment,
which almost all sons of shepherds do, whether they
adhere to herding sheep in after-life or not.   Seasons
and emergencies not seldom occur when the aid
which the little boy can lend often proves not much
less availing than that of the grown-up man.   Educa-

* A flock of sheep.

tion in this line consequently commences early. A knowledge of the habits, together with the proper treatment of sheep, and therefore of pastoral affairs in general, 'grows with the growth' of the individual, and becomes, as it were, a portion of his nature. I had thus assisted my father more or less all along; and when a little older, though still a mere boy, I went for a year to a friend at Glencotha, in Holmswater, as assistant shepherd or lamb-herd. Another year in the same capacity I was with a shepherd in Wester Buccleuch. It was at Glencotha that I first made a sustained attempt to compose in rhyme. When in Wester Buccleuch my life was much more lonely, and became more tinged with thoughts and feelings of a romantic cast. Owing to the nature of the stock kept on the farm, it was my destiny day after day to be out among the mountains during the whole summer season from early morn till the fall of even. But the long summer days, whether clear or cloudy, never seemed long to me—I never wearied among the wilds. My flocks being *hirsled*, as it is expressed, required vigilance; but, if this was judiciously maintained, the task was for the most part an easy and pleasant one. I know not if it be worth while to mention that the hills and glens on which my charge pastured at this period formed a portion of what in ancient times was termed the Forest of Rankleburn. The names of places in the district, though there were no other more intelligible traditions, might serve to show that it is a range of country to which both kings and nobles had resorted. If from morning to night I was away far from the homes of living men, I was not so in regard to those of the dead. Where a lesser stream from the wild uplands comes down and meets the Rankleburn, a church or chapel once stood, surrounded, like most other consecrated places of the kind, by a burial-ground. There tradition says that five dukes, some say kings, lie buried under a marble stone. I had heard that Sir Walter, then Mr Scott, had, a number of years previously, made a pilgrimage to this place, for the purpose of discovering the sepulchres of the great and nearly forgotten dead, but without success. This, however, tended, in my estimation, to confirm the truth of the tradition; and having enough of time and opportunity, I made many a toilsome effort of a similar nature, with the same result. With hills around, wild and rarely trodden, and the ceaseless yet ever-varying tinkling of its streams, together with the mysterious echoes which the least stir seemed to awaken, the place was not only lonely, but also creative of strange apprehensions, even in the hours of open day. It is strange that the heart will fear the dead, which, perhaps, never feared the living. Though I could muster and maintain courage to dig perseveringly among the dust of the long-departed when the sun shone in the sky, yet when the shadow of night was coming, or had come down upon the earth, the scene was sacredly secure from all inroad on my part; and, to make the matter sufficiently intelligible, I may further mention that, some years afterwards, when I took a fancy one evening to travel eight miles to meet some friends in a shepherd's lone muirland dwelling, I made the way somewhat longer for the sake of evading the impressive loneliness of this locality. I had no belief that I should meet accusing spirits of the dead; but I disliked to be troubled in waging war with those *eerie* feelings which are the offspring of superstitious associations.

"While a lamb-herd at Buccleuch, I read when I could get a book which was not already threadbare. I had a few chisels, and files, and other tools, with which I took pleasure in constructing, of wood or bone, pieces of mechanism; and I kept a diary, in which I wrote many minute and trivial matters, as well, no doubt, as I then thought, many a sage observation. In this, likewise, I wrote rude rhymes on local occurrences. But I have anticipated a little. On returning home from Glencotha, and two years before I went to Buccleuch, a younger brother and I had still another round at herding cattle, which pastured in a park near by my father's cottage. Our part was to protect a meadow which formed a portion of it ; and the task being easy to protect that for which the cattle did not much care, nor yet could skaithe greatly though they should trespass upon it, we were far too idle not to enter upon and prosecute many a wayward and unprofitable ploy. Our predilections for taming wild birds— the wilder by nature the better—seemed boundless ; and our family of hawks, and owls, and ravens, was too large not to cost us much toil, anxiety, and even sorrow. We fished in the Ettrick and the lesser streams. These last suited our way of it best, since we generally fished with staves and plough-spades— thus far, at least, honourably giving the objects of our pursuit a fair chance of escape. When the hay had been won, we went to Ettrick school, at which we continued throughout the winter, travelling to and from it daily, though it lay at the distance of five miles. This we, in good weather, accomplished conveniently enough ; but it proved occasionally a serious and toilsome task through wind and rain, or keen frost and deep snow, when winter days and the mountain blasts came on.

"My father, after being three years in Stanhope-foot, on the banks of the Ettrick, went to Deloraine-shiels, an *out-bye herding*, under the same employer. In the winter season either I or some other of the family assisted him ; but so often as the weather was fine, we went to a school instituted by a farmer in the neighbourhood for behoof of his own family. When by-and-by I went to herd the *hirsel* which my father formerly tended, like most other regular shepherds I delighted in and was proud of the employment. A considerable portion of another *hirsel* lying contiguous, and which my elder brother herded, was for the summer season of the year added to mine, so that this already large was made larger; but exempted as I was from attending to aught else but my flock, I had pleasant days, for I loved the wilds among which it had become alike my destiny and duty to walk at will. The hills of Ettrick are generally wild and green, and those of them on which I daily wandered, musing much and writing often, were as high, green, and wild as any of them all.

" According to my ability I studied while wandering among the mountains, and at intervals, adopting my knee for my desk, wrote down the results of my musing. Let not the shepherd ever forget his dog —his constant companion and best friend, and without which all his efforts would little avail! Mine knew well the places where in my rounds I was wont to pause, and especially the majestic seat which I occupied so often on the loftiest peak of Stanhope-law. It had also an adopted spot of rest the while, and, confident of my habits, would fold itself down upon it ere I came forward, and would linger still, look wistful, and marvel why if at any time I passed on without making my wonted delay.

" In rural, as well as in other life, there are things said and done which are more or less ungenerous. These, if at any time they came my way, I repelled as best I might. But I did not stop here ; whether such matters, when occurring, might concern myself as an individual or not, I took it upon me, as if I had been a ' learned judge,' to write satires upon such persons as I knew or conceived to have spoken or acted in aught contrary to good manners. These squibs were written through the impulse of offended feeling, or the stirrings of that injudicious spirit which sometimes prompts a man to exercise a power merely because he possesses it. They were still, after all, only as things of private experiment, and not intended ever to go forth to the world, though it happened otherwise. I usually carried a lot of these writings in my hat ; and by-and-by, unlike most other young authors, I got a publisher unsought for. This was the wind, which, on a wild day, swept my hat from my head, and, tattering its contents asunder from their fold, sent them away over hill and dale like a flock of wildfowl. I recovered some where they had halted in bieldy places ; others of them went further, and fell into other hands, and particularly into those of a neighbour, who, a short while previously, had played an unmanly part relating to a sheep and the march which ran between us. He found his unworthy proceeding boldly discussed in an epistle which, I daresay, no other carrier would ever have conveyed to him but the unblushing mountain blast. He complained to others, whom he found more or less involved in his own predicament, and the thing went disagreeably abroad. My master, through good taste and feeling, was vexed, as I understood, that I should have done anything that gave ground for accusation, though he did not mention the subject to myself; but my father, some days after the mischief had commenced, came to me upon the hill, and, not in very good humour, disapproved of my imprudent conduct. As for the consequences of this untoward event, it proved the means of revealing what I had hitherto concealed—procuring for me a sort of local popularity little to be envied. I made the best improvement of it, as I then thought, that lay in my power—by writing a satire upon myself.

"I continued shepherd at Deloraine two years, and then went in the same capacity to the late Mr Knox of Todrigg; and if at the former place I had been well and happy, here I was still more so. His son William, the poet of the 'The Lonely Hearth,' paid me much friendly attention. He commended

my verses, and augured my success as one of the
song-writers of my native land. In those days I
did not write with the most remote view to publication. My aim did not extend beyond the gratifi-
cation of hearing my mountain strains sung by lad
or lass as time and place might favour. And when,
in the dewy gloaming of a summer eve, returning
home from the hill, and when 'the kye were in the
loan,' I did hear this much, I thought, no doubt, that

> 'The swell and fall of these wild tones
> Were worth the pomp of a thousand thrones.'

"My fortune in life had not placed me within
the reach of a library, and I had read almost
none; and although I had attempted to write, I
merely followed the course which instinct pointed
out. Need I state further, that if in these days I
employed my mind and pen among the mountains
as much as possible, my thoughts also often continued to pursue the same practice, even when
among others, by the 'farmer's ingle.' I retired to
rest when others retired, but if not outworn by
matters of extra toil, the ardour of thought, through
love of the poet's undying art, would, night after
night, for many hours, debar the inroads of sleep.
The number of schools which I have particularised
as having attended may occasion some surprise at
the deficiency of my scholarship. For this, various
reasons are assignable, all of which, however, hinge

upon these two formidable obstacles — the inconveniency of local position, and the thoughtless inattention of youth. In remote country places, long and rough ways, conjoined not unfrequently with wild weather, require that children, before they can enter school, be pretty well grown up; consequently, they quit it the sooner. They are often useful at home in the summer season, or circumstances may destine them to hire away. Among these inconveniences, one serious drawback is, that the little education they do get is rarely obtained continuously, and regular progress is interrupted. Much of what has been gained is lost during the intervals of non-attendance, and every new return to the book is little else than a new beginning. So was it with me. At the time when my father hired a teacher into his house it was for what is termed the winter quarter, and I was then somewhat too young to be tied down to the regular routine of school discipline ; and if older when boarded away, the other obstruction to salutary progress began to operate grievously against me. I acquired bit by bit the common education—reading, writing, and arithmetic. So far as I remember, grammar was not much taught at any of these schools, and the spelling of words was very nearly as little attended to as the meaning which they are appointed to convey was explained or sought after.

" And then, in regard to books, as of these I rarely got more than might serve as a whet to the appetite, I might have the desire of those whose longings after what they would obtain are increased by the difficulties which interpose between them and the possession. One book which in school I sometimes got a glance of, I would have given anything to possess : this was a small volume entitled, ' The Three Hundred Animals.'

" I cannot forbear mentioning that, when at Deloraine, I was greatly advantaged by an old woman, called Mary Hogg, whose cottage stood on an isolated corner of the lands on which my flock pastured. Her husband had been a shepherd, who, many years previous to this period, perished in a snow-storm. In her youth she had opportunities of reading history and other literature, and she did not only remember what she had read, but could give a distinct and interesting account of it. In going my wonted rounds, few days there were on which I did not call and listen to her intelligent conversation. She was a singularly good woman—a sincere Christian ; and the books which she lent me were generally of a religious kind, such as the ' Pilgrim's Progress ' and the ' Holy War ;' but here I also discovered a romance, the first which I had ever seen. It was printed in the Gothic letter, and entitled ' Prissimus, the renowned Prince of Bohemia.'. Particular scenes and characters in 'Ivanhoe' remind me strikingly of those I had formerly met with in this old book of black print. And I must mention that few books interested me more than 'Bailey's Dictionary.' Day after day I bore it to the mountains, and I have an impression that it was a more comprehensive edition of the work than I have ever since been able to meet with.

"At Todrigg my reading was extended; and having begun more correctly to appreciate what I did read, the intention which I had sometimes entertained gathered strength : this was to make an effort to obtain a regular education. The consideration of the inadequacy of my means had hitherto bridled my ambition; but having herded as a regular shepherd nearly three years, during which I had no occasion to spend much of my income, my prospects behoved to be a little more favourable. It was in this year that the severest trial which had yet crossed my path had to be sustained. The death of my father overthrew my happier mood; at the same time, instead of subduing my secret aim, the event rather strengthened my determination. My portion of my father's worldly effects added something considerable to my own gainings; and, resigning my situation, I bade farewell to the crook and plaid." Mr Riddell states that he then entered the parish school of Biggar, in Clydesdale, where his teacher, "the late Richard Scott, was an accurate classical scholar, and free from pedantry. He was kind-hearted, and somewhat disposed to indolence, loving more to converse with one of my years than to instruct him in languages. He had seen a good deal of the world and its ways, and I learned much from him besides Greek and Latin. We were great friends and companions, and rarely separate when both of us were unengaged otherwise."

"I bore aloof from making many acquaintances; yet ere long I became pretty extensively acquainted with the people of the place. It went abroad that I was a bard from the mountains, and the rumour affixed to me a popularity which I did not enjoy.

"It was about this time that I wrote 'The Crook and Plaid'—not by request, but with the intention of supplanting a song, I think of English origin, called 'The Ploughboy,' and of a somewhat questionable character. 'The Crook and Plaid' accomplished the end intended, and soon became popular throughout the land. So soon as I got a glimpse of the Roman language, I began to make satisfactory progress in its acquisition. But I daily wrote more or less in my old way, now also embracing in my attempts prose as well as verse. I wrote a 'Border Romance.' This was more strongly than correctly expressed. I contributed some papers to the 'Clydesdale Magazine,' and I sent a sort of poetic tale to the editor, telling him to do with it whatever he might think proper. He published it anonymously, and it was sold about Clydesdale.

"I had become acquainted with a number of people whom I delighted to visit occasionally; one family in particular, who lived amid the beauty of 'the wild glen sae green.' The song now widely known by this name I wrote for a member of this delightful family, who at that time herded one of the *hirsels* of his father's flocks on the 'heathy hill.' With the greater number of persons in the district possessing literary tastes I became more or less intimate. The schoolmasters I found friendly and obliging; one of these, in particular (now holding a higher office in the same locality), I often visited. His high poetic taste convinced me more and more of the value of mental culture, and tended to subdue me from those more rugged modes of expression in which I took a pride in conveying my conceptions. With this interesting friend I sometimes took excursions into rural regions more or less remote, and once we journeyed to the south, when I had the pleasure of introducing him to the Ettrick Shepherd. But of my acquaintances, I valued few more than my modest and poetic friend, the late James Brown of Symington.* Though humble in station, he was high in virtuous worth. His mind, imbued with

* See "Modern Scottish Minstrel," vol. iii. p. 186.

and regulated by sound religious and moral principle, was as ingenious and powerful as his heart was 'leal, warm, and kind.'

"Entering the University of Edinburgh, I took for the first session the Greek and Latin classes. Attending them regularly, I performed the incumbent exercises much after the manner that others did— only, as I have always understood it to be a rare thing with the late Mr Dunbar, the Greek Professor, to give much praise to anything in the shape of poetry, I may mention that marked merit was ascribed to me in his class for a poetical translation of one of the odes of Anacreon. I had laid the translation on his desk, in an anonymous state, one day before the assembling of the class. He read it and praised it, expressing at the same time his anxiety to know who was the translator; but the translator having intended not to acknowledge it, kept quiet. He returned to it, and, praising it anew, expressed still more earnestly his desire to know the author; and so I made myself known, as all *great unknowns*, I think, with the exception of Junius, are sooner or later destined to do.

"Of the philosophical classes, those that I liked best were the logic and moral philosophy, particularly the latter. I have often thought that it is desirable, could it be possibly found practicable, to have all the teachers of the higher departments of education not merely of high scholastic acquirements, but of acknowledged genius. Youth reveres genius, and delights to be influenced by it; heart and spirit are kept awake and refreshed by it, and everything connected with its forthgivings is rendered doubly memorable. It fixes, in a certain sense, the limit of expectation; and the prevailing sentiment is—we are under the tuition of the highest among those on earth who teach; if we do not profit here, we may not hope to do so elsewhere. These remarks I make with a particular reference to the late Professor Wilson, under the influence of whose genius and generous warmth of heart many have felt as I was wont to feel. If it brings hope and gladness to love and esteem the living, it also yields a satisfaction, though mingled with regret, to venerate the dead; and now that he is no more, I cannot forbear recording how he treated a man from the mountains who possessed no previous claim upon his attention. I had no introduction to him, but he said that he had heard of me, and would accept of no fee for his class when I joined it; at least he would not do so, he said, till I should be able to inform him whether or not I had been pleased with his lectures. But it proved all the same in this respect at the close as it was at the commencement of the session. He invited me frequently to his house as a friend, when other friends were to meet him there, besides requesting me to come and see him and his family whenever I could make it convenient. I thus became possessed of a privilege of which I did not fail to avail myself frequently—a privilege which might well have been gratifying to such as were much less enthusiastic with regard to literary men and things than I was. To share in the conversation of those possessed of high literary taste and talent, and, above all, of poetic genius, is the highest enjoyment afforded by society ; and if it be thus gratifying, it is almost unnecessary to add that it is also advantageous in no ordinary degree, if, indeed, properly appreciated and improved. Any one who ever met the late Professor in the midst of his own happy family, constituted as it was when I had this pleasure, was not likely soon to forget a scene wherein so much genius, kindness, loveliness, and worth were blended. If the world does not think with a deep and undying regret of what once adorned it, and it has now lost, through the intervention of those shadows which no morning but the eternal one can remove, I am one, at least, who in this respect cannot follow its example.

"Edinburgh, with its 'palaces and towers,' and its many crowded ways, was at first strangely new to me, being as different, in almost all respects, to what I had been accustomed as it might seem possible for contrariety to make earthly things. Though I had friends in it, and therefore was not solitary, yet its tendency, like that of the noisy and restless sea, was to render me melancholy. Some features which the congregated condition of mankind exhibited penetrated my heart with something like actual dismay. I had seen nothing of the sort, nor yet even so much as a semblance of it, and therefore I had no idea that there existed such a miserable shred of degradation, for example, as a cinder-woman—desolate and dirty as her employment—bowed down—a shadow among shadows—busily prone, beneath the sheety night sky, to find out and fasten upon the crumb, whose pilgrimage certainly had not improved it since falling from the rich man's table. Compassion, though not naturally so, becomes painful when entertained towards those whom we believe labouring under suffering which we fain would but cannot alleviate.

" I had enough of curiosity for wishing to see all those things which others spoke of, and characterised as worthy of being seen; but I contented myself meanwhile with a survey of the city's external attributes. In a week or two, however, my friend, A. F. Harrower, having come into town from Clydesdale, took pleasure in finding out whatever could interest or gratify me, and of conveying me thither. Through his persevering attentions towards me, I met with much agreeable society, and saw much above as well as somewhat below the earth, which I

might never otherwise have seen. In illustration of
the latter fact, I may state that, having gone to
London, he returned with two Englishmen, when
he invited me to assist them in exploring the battle-
field of Pinkie. We terminated our excursion by
descending one of Sir John Hope's coal-pits. These
humorous and frank English associates amused
themselves by bantering my friend and myself about
the chastisement which Scotland received from the
sister kingdom at Pinkie. As did the young rustic
countryman—or, at least, was admonished to do—
so did I. When going away to reside in England,
he asked his father if he had any advice to give him.
'Nane, Jock, nane but this,' he said; 'dinna forget
to avenge the battle o' Pinkie on them.' Ere I slept
I wrote, in support of our native land, the song—
'Ours is the land of gallant hearts;' and thus, in my
own way, 'avenged the battle of Pinkie.'

"One of two friends with whom I delighted to
associate was Robert Barton, an early school companion, who, having left the mountains earlier than
I did, had now been a number of years in Edinburgh.
Of excellent head and generous heart, he loved the
wild, green, and deep solitudes of nature. The
other, George Macdonald, was of powerful and bold
intellect, and remarkable for a retentive memory.
Each of us, partial to those regions where nature
strives to maintain her own undisturbed dominion,

on all holidays hied away from the city, to the woodland and mountainous haunts, or the loneliness of the least-frequented shores of the sea. The spirit of our philosophy varied much—sometimes profound and solemn, and sometimes humorous; but still we philosophised, wandering on. They were members of a literary society which met once a-week, and which I joined. My propensity to study character and note its varieties was here afforded a field opening close upon me; but I was also much profited by performing my part in carrying forward the business of the institution. During all the sessions that I attended the University, but especially as these advanced toward their termination, I entered into society beyond that which might be regarded as professionally literary. I had an idea then, as I still have, that, in every process of improvement, care should be taken that one department of our nature is not cultivated to the neglect of another. There are two departments—the intellectual and the moral; the one implying all that is rational, the other comprising whatever pertains to feeling and passion—or, more simply, there are the head and the heart ; and if the intellect is to be cultivated, the heart is not to be allowed to run into wild waste, nor to sink into systematic apathy.

"My last year's attendance at the College Philosophical Classes was at St Andrews. I had a craving to acquaint myself with a city noted in story, and I could not, under the canopy of my native sky, have planted the step among scenes more closely inter-woven with past national transactions, or fraught with more interesting associations.

"The ruins which intermingle with the scenery and happy homes of St Andrews, like grey hairs among those of another hue, rendered venerable the general aspect of the place. But I did not feel only the city interesting, but the whole of Fifeshire. By excursions made on the monthly holidays then as well as subsequently, when in after-years I returned to visit friends in the royal realm, I acquainted myself with a goodly number of those haunts and scenes which history and tradition have rendered attractive.

"I studied at St Andrews College under the late Dr Jackson, who was an eminent philosopher and friendly man ; also under Mr Duncan, of the Mathe-matical Chair, whom I regarded as a personification of unworldly simplicity, clothed in high and pure thought ; and I regularly attended, though not en-rolled as a regular student, the Moral Philosophy Class of Dr Chalmers. Returning to Edinburgh and its University, I became acquainted, through my friend and countryman Robert Hogg, with R. A. Smith, who was desirous that I should assist him with the works in which he was engaged, particularly

'The Irish Minstrel' and 'Select Melodies.' Smith was a man of modest worth and superior intelligence; peculiarly delicate in his taste and feeling in everything pertaining to lyric poetry as well as music; his criticisms were strict, and, as some thought, unnecessarily minute. Diffident and retiring, he was not got acquainted with at once; but when he gave his confidence, he was found a pleasant companion and warm-hearted friend. If, as he had sought my acquaintance, I might have expected more frankness on our meeting, I soon became convinced that his shyer cast arose alone from excess of modesty, combined with a remarkable sensitiveness of feeling. Proudly honourable, he seemed more susceptible of the influences of all sorts that affect life than any man I ever knew; and, indeed, a little acquaintance with him was only required to show that his harp was strung too delicately for standing long the tear and wear of this world. He had done much for Scottish melody, both by fixing the old airs in as pure a state as possible, and by adding to the vast number of these national treasures some exquisite airs of his own. For a number of the airs in the works just mentioned, but particularly in the 'Select Melodies,' he had experienced difficulty in procuring suitable words, owing chiefly to the crampness of the measures—a serious drawback, which appears to pervade, more or less, the sweetest

melodies of other nations as well as those of our own.
A number of these I supplied as well as I could.

"About this time the native taste for Scottish
song in city society seemed nearly if not altogether
lost, and a kind of songs, such as 'I've been roam-
ing,' 'I'd be a butterfly,' 'Buy a broom,' 'Cherry
ripe,' &c. (in which if the head contrived to find a
meaning, it was still such as the heart could under-
stand nothing about), seemed alone to be popular,
and to prevail. R. A. Smith disliked this state of
things, but, perhaps, few more so than Mr P.
M'Leod, who gave a most splendid evidence of his
taste in his 'Original National Melodies.' Both
Smith and M'Leod were very particular about the
quality of the poetry which they honoured with
their music. M'Leod was especially careful in this
respect. He loved the lay of lofty and undaunted
feeling as well as of love and friendship; for his
genius is of a manly tone, and has a bold and liberal
flow. And popular as some of the effusions in his
work have become, such as 'Oh! why left I my
hame?' and 'Scotland yet!' many others of them,
I am convinced, will yet be popular likewise. When
the intelligence of due appreciation draws towards
them, it will take them up and delight to fling them
upon the breezes that blow over the hills and glens,
and among the haunts and homes of the isle of
unconquerable men. To Mr M'Leod's 'National

Melodies' I contributed a number of songs. In the composition of these I found it desirable to lay aside, in some considerable degree, my pastoral phraseology, for, as conveyed in such productions, I observed that city society cared little about rural scenery and sentiment. It was different with my kind and gifted friend Professor Wilson. He was wont to say that he would not have given the education, as he was pleased to term it, which I had received afar in the green bosom of mountain solitude, and among the haunts and homes of the shepherd—meaning the thing as applicable to poetry—for all that he had received at colleges. Wilson had introduced my song, 'When the glen all is still,' into the *Noctes*, and La Sapio composed music for it; and not only was it sung in Drury Lane, but published in a sheet as the production of a real shepherd; yet it did not become popular in city life. In the country it had been popular previous to this, where it is so still, and where no effort whatever had been made to introduce it.

" About the time when I had concluded the whole of my college course, the 'Songs of the Ark '* were published by Blackwood. These, as published, are not what they were at first, and were intended only to be short songs of a sacred nature, unconnected by intervening narrative, for which R. A. Smith

* "Songs of the Ark, with other Poems." Edin. 1831. 8vo.

wished to compose music.   Unfortunately, his other
manifold engagements never permitted him to carry
his intention into practice ; and seeing no likelihood
of any decrease of these engagements, I gave scope
to my thoughts on the subject, and the work became
what it now is.   But I ought to mention that this
was not my first poetic publication in palpable
shape.   Some years previously I published stanzas,
or a monody, on the death of Lord Byron.   I had
all along thought much, and with something like
mysterious awe, upon the eccentric temperament,
character, and history of that great poet, and the
tidings which told the event of his demise impressed
me deeply.   Being in the country, and remote from
those who could exchange thoughts with me on the
occurrence, I resorted to writing.   That which I
advanced was much mixed up with the result, if I
I may not say of former experience, yet of former
reflection, for I had entertained many conjectures
concerning what this powerful personage would or
might yet do; and, indeed, his wilful waywardness,
together with the misery which he represented as
continually haunting him, constituted an impressive
advertisement to the world, and served to keep
human attention awake towards him.

" The summer vacations of college year I passed
in the country, sometimes residing with my mother
and eldest brother at a small farm which he occu-

pied at the foot of the Lammermuir Hills, in East
Lothian, called Brookside; and sometimes, when I
wished a variety, with another brother, at Dryden,
in Selkirkshire. At both places I had enough of
time, not only for study, but also for what I may
call amusement. The latter consisted in various
literary projects which I entered upon, but particularly those of a poetic kind, and the writing of letters
to friends, with whom I regularly, and I may say
also copiously, corresponded; for in these we did not
merely express immediate thoughts and feelings of a
more personal nature, but remarked with vigorous
frankness upon many standard affairs of this scene
of things. To this general rule of the manner of
my life at this time, however, I must mention an
exception. A college companion and I, thinking to
advantage ourselves, and perhaps others, took a
school at Fisherrow. The speculation in the end,
as to money matters, served us nothing. It was
easier to get scholars than to get much, if anything,
for teaching them. Yet neither was the former, in
some respects, so easy as might have been expected.
The offspring of man, in that locality, may be regarded as in some measure amphibious. Boys and
girls equally, if not already in the sea, were like
young turtles, sure to be pointing towards it with
an instinct too intense to err. I never met, indeed,
with a race of beings believed or even suspected to

be rational, that, provided immediate impulses and
inclinations could be gratified, cared so thoroughly
little for consequences. On warm summer days,
when we caused the school-door to stand open, it
is not easy to say how much intense interest this
simple circumstance drew towards it. The squint of
the unsettled eye was on the door, out at which the
heart and all its inheritance was off and away long
previously, and the more than ordinarily propitious
moment for the limbs following was only as yet not
arrived. When that moment came, off went one,
followed by another, and down the narrow and dark
lanes of sooty houses. As well might the steps have
proposed to pursue meteors playing at hide-and-seek
among the clouds of a midnight sky that the tempest
was troubling. Nevertheless, Colin Bell, who, by
virtue of his ceaseless stir in the exercise of his hea-
then-god-like abilities, had constituted himself cap-
tain of the detective band, would be up and at hand
immediately, and would say, ' Master—sir, Young
an' me will bring them, sir, if ye'll let's.' It was
just as good to ' let' as to hinder, for, for others to
be out thus, and he in, seemed to be an advantage
gained over Colin to which he could never be rightly
reconciled. He was bold and frank, and full of expedients in cases of emergency ; especially he appeared capable of rendering more reasons for an error
in his conduct than one could well have imagined

could have been rendered for anything done in life
below. Another drawback in the case was, that one
could never be very seriously angry with him. If
more real than pretended at any time, his broad
bright eye and bluff face, magnificently lifted up,
like the sun on frost-work, melted down displeasure,
and threatened to betray all the policy depending
on it; for in the main never a bit of ill heart had
Colin, though doubtlessly he had in him, deeply
established, a train of rebellion against education that
seemed ever on the alert, and which repulsed even
its portended approach with a vigour resembling the
electric energy of the torpedo.

"As we did not much like this place, we did not
remain long in it.

"I have dwelt at the greater length on these
matters, trivial though they be, in consequence of
my non-intention of tracing minutely the steps and
stages of my probationary career. These, with me,
I suppose, were much like what they are and have
been with others. My acquaintance was a little extended with those that inhabit the land, and in some
cases a closer intimacy than mere acquaintance took
place, and more lasting friendships were formed.

"My brother having taken the farm of Ramsaycleugh-
burn, near Teviothead, I left Brookside; and as all the
members of the family were wont to account that in
which my mother lived their home, it of course was

mine. But, notwithstanding that the change brought me almost to the very border of the vale of my nativity, I regretted to leave Brookside. It was a beautiful and interesting place, and the remembrance of it is like what Ossian says of joys that are past—'sweet and mournful to the soul.' I loved the place, was partial to the peacefulness of its retirement, its solitude, and the intelligence of its society. I was near the laird's library, and I had a garden in the glen. The latter was formed that I might gather home to it, when in musing moods among the mountains, the wild-flowers, in order to their cultivation, and my having something more of a possessory right over them. It formed a contrast to the scenery around, and lured to relaxation. Occasionally 'the lovely of the land' brought, with industrious delight, plants and flowers, that they might have a share in adorning it. Even when I was from home, it was, upon the whole, well attended to ; for although, according to taste or caprice, changes were made, yet I readily forgave the annoyances that might attend alteration, and especially those by the hands that sometimes printed me pleasing compliments on the clay with the little stones lifted from the walks. If the things which I have written and given to the world, or may yet give, continue to be cared for, these details may not be wholly without use, inasmuch as they will serve to explain frequent allusions which might otherwise seem introduced at capricious random, or made without a meaning.

Shortly after becoming a probationer, I came to reside in this district,* and not long after, the preacher who officiated in the preaching station here died. The people connected with it wished me to become his successor, which, after some difficulties on their part had been surmounted, I became. I had other views at the time which were promising and important; but as there had been untoward disturbances in the place, owing to the lack of defined rights and privileges, I had it in my power to become a peacemaker; and, beside, I felt it my duty to comply with a call which was both cordial and unanimous. I now laid wholly aside those things which pertain to the pursuits of romantic literature, and devoted myself to the performance of incumbent duties. In consequence of no house having been provided for the preacher, and no one to be obtained but at a very inconvenient distance, I was in this respect very inconveniently situated. Travelling nine miles to the scene of my official duties, it was frequently my lot to preach in a very uncomfortable condition, when, indeed, the wet would be pouring from my arms on the Bible before me, and oozing over my shoes when the foot was stirred on the pulpit floor. But, by-

* This was written at Teviothead.

and-by, the Duke of Buccleuch built a dwelling-house for me, the same which I still occupy.

" In the hope of soon obtaining a permanent and comfortable settlement at Teviothead, I had ventured to make my own, by marriage, her who had in heart been mine through all my college years, and who for my sake had, in the course of these, rejected wealth and high standing in life. The heart that, for the sake of leal faith and love, could despise wealth and its concomitants, and brave the risk of embracing comparative poverty, even at its best estate, was not one likely overmuch to fear that poverty when it appeared, nor flinch with an altered tone from the position which it had adopted, when it actually came. This, much rather, fell to my part. It preyed upon my mind too deeply not to prove injurious in its effects ; and it did this all the more, that the voice of love, true to its own law, had the words of hope and consolation in it, but never those of complaint. It appeared the *acmé* of the severity of fate itself to have lived to be the mean of placing a heart and mind so rich in disinterested affection on so wild and waste a scene of trial.

" From an experience of fourteen years, in which there were changes in almost all things except in the affection which bound two hearts in one before the hands were united, it might be expected that I should give some eminent admonitions concerning the im-

prudence of men, and particularly of students, allow-
ing their hearts to become interested in, and the
remembrance of their minds more fraught with, the
rich beauty of auburn ringlets than in the untoward
confusion, for example, of irregular Greek verbs ; yet
I much fear that admonition would be of no use.
If their fate be woven of a texture similar to that of
mine, how can they help it ? A man may have an
idea that to cling to the shelter which he has found,
and indulge in the sleep that has overtaken him
amid the stormy blasts of the waste mountains, may
be little else than opening for himself the gates of
death, yet the toils of the way through which he has
already passed may also have rendered him incapable
of resisting the dangerous rest and repose of his immediate accommodation. In regard to my own love
affairs, I, throughout all these long years which I
have specified, might well have adopted, as the motto
of both mind and heart, these lines——

> ' Oh, poortith cauld and restless love,
>   Ye wreck my peace between ye.'

I had, as has already been hinted, a rival, who, if
not so devotedly attached as I, nevertheless was by
far too much so for any one who is destined to love
without encouragement. He was as rich in proportion as I was poor. The gifts of love, called the
gifts of friendship, which he contrived to bestow

were costly; mine, as fashioned forth by a higher
hand than that of art, might be equally rich and
beautiful in the main, yet wild-flowers, though yel-
low as the gold, and, though wrapped in rhymes,
are light ware when weighed against the solid material. He, in personal appearance, manners, and
generosity of heart, was one with whom it was impossible to be acquainted and not to esteem; and
another feature of this affair was, that we were
friends, and almost constant companions for some
years. When in the country I had to be with him
as continually as possible; and when I went to the
city, it was his wont to follow me. Here, then, was
a web strangely woven by the fingers of a wayward
fate. Feelings were brought into daily exercise which
might seem the least compatible with being brought
into contact and maintained in harmony. And these
things, which are strictly true, if set forth in the
contrivances of romance, might, or in all likelihood
would, be pronounced unnatural or overstrained. The
worth and truth of the heart to which these fond
anxieties related left me no ground to fear for losing
that regard which I valued as ' light and life' itself;
but in another way there reached me a matchless
misery, and which haunted me almost as constantly
as my own shadow when the sun shone. Consider-
ing the dark uncertainty of my future prospects in
life, that regard I felt it fearful almost beyond mea-

sure even to seek to retain, incurring the responsibility of marring the fortune of one whom nevertheless I could not bear the thought of another than myself having the bliss of rendering blessed. If selfishness be thus seen to exist even in love itself, I would fain hope that it is of an elevated and peculiar kind, and not that which grovels, dragging downwards, and therefore justly deserving of the name. I am the more anxious in regard to this on account of its being in my own case felt so deeply. It maintained its ground with more or less firmness at all times, and ultimately triumphed, in despite of all efforts made to the contrary, over the suggestions of prudence and even the sterner reasonings of the sense of justice. In times of sadness and melancholy, which, like the preacher's days of darkness, were many, when hope scarcely lit the gloom of the heart on which it sat though the band of love was about its brow, I busied myself in endeavouring to form resolutions to resign my pretensions to the warmer regard of her who was the object of all this serious solicitude; but neither she herself, nor time and place, seemed, so far as I could see, disposed in the least to aid me in these efforts of self control and denial; and, indeed, even at best, I much suspect that the resolutions of lovers in such cases are only like the little dams which the rivulet forms in itself by the frail material of stray grass-piles and wild-rose leaves, easily overturned by the next slight impulse that the wave receives.

" Notwithstanding the ever-living solicitude and sad suffering constituting the keen and trying experience of many years, as arising in consequence of this attachment and untoward circumstances, it has brought more than a sufficient compensation; and were it possible, and the choice given, I would assuredly follow the same course, and suffer it all over again, rather than be without ' that treasure of departed sorrow ' that is even now at my right hand as I write these lines."

Mr Riddell continued to perform the duties of minister of Teviothead, with much acceptance to the people over whom he was placed, and with great satisfaction to himself, although he had many disadvantages to contend with, up till 1841, when he became the subject, like some other distinguished poets before him, of an attack of that most dreadful of all maladies—insanity. In May, of that year, his mind had become so much disordered, that it was deemed advisable to place him in the Crichton Royal Institution at Dumfries, where he was a patient of that accomplished physician Dr W. A. F. Browne, who has kindly furnished the following most interesting and valuable narrative of his case:—

" The origin of his malady was traced to the circulation of a report, calculated, if not to impair the usefulness of his ministrations, to wound his feelings at the most sensitive point. The injury inflicted produced at first great distress of mind, which might fairly be regarded as the natural result of such a crisis in a mind so constituted; but what was at first merely anxiety and dejection, gradually passed into panic and perplexity, until the suggestions of his naturally emotional and imaginative disposition, escaping from the control of reason, gradually assumed the form of substantive delusions, or of delusive fears. Either as an effect of treatment or the natural subsidence of his agitation, greater equanimity and self-possession were observed, greater confidence and reliance were extended to me, and the misconceptions by which he had been enslaved were either doubted, or exercised less dominion over his imagination; but although the phantom conspiracies, &c., by which he had been haunted, had faded in distinctness, the incontrollable apprehension and anxiety remained in full force. He was terror-stricken, but could not identify nor describe the objects of his fear.

" He was designedly placed as a member of a group consisting of two clergymen, two literateurs by profession, a medical man, and several other individuals of education and cultivated tastes, in the hope that the sympathies, similarity of pursuit, and habits of thought, might engage his attention, and prove a

source at once of distraction and consolation; but at
no period of his residence did he enter into intimate
relations with his companions, or do more than
tolerate the intercourse and genuine kindness of
which he was the object. This isolation proceeded
rather from shyness, and a suspicion that his
country bearing and local reputation scarcely entitled him to a defined position in such a com-
munity. To me he was as open and candid as his
quiet and unobtrusive nature permitted. I served
as a confessor for his sorrows and secret cogitations,
and these revelations were sometimes of a most
startling but interesting character. His principal
theme was naturally the misery and suffering by
which he was bowed down; but he likewise dwelt
upon his inability to escape from these tyrannical
feelings, upon the utter change which appeared to
have taken place in not only his own family and
social relations, but even in the external face of the
world; and upon a suspicion either that his original
identity had been subverted, or that a duality of
consciousness had been established by the processes
of disease. He spoke much of two parallel cur-
rents of thought which seemed to run constantly
through his mind, one of these consisting of suggestions of despondency and despair, the other of
bright imaginings, which shaped themselves into
couplets, or verses of some description. He appeared

to be convinced that many of these trains of ideas, especially the composition of poetry, originated outside or beyond himself, that neither the thoughts nor their expression nor the rhymes were acts of volition, or could have been prevented or altered had he so wished. He repeated specimens of these productions, and they were precisely of the same character as those which I afterwards learned to recognise as his. They consisted of lyrics, Border ballads, hymns, and excited my wonder and admiration, both by their beauty and sweetness, and by their origin in a mind so darkened and disturbed, and amid such exquisite pain and terror. It is very probable that the atmosphere in which he lived—in other words, the conversations which he heard, the books and manuscripts and occupations of his associates—might have insensibly suggested recurrence to his former mental pursuits and sources of happiness, for at this time every effort was made to induce my patients to engage in literary work ; and so successful was the attempt that now were produced many of those poems, essays, 'quips and cranks and wanton wiles,' which in after years appeared in the pages of the 'New Moon,' and were at that distant time regarded as marvellous illustrations of the possibility of eliciting light from darkness,

> ' Darkness shows us worlds of light
> We never saw by day,'

and of employing in a natural manner the healthy faculties of morbid minds. Mr Riddell contributed largely to its pages, and many of his poems can still be pointed out; but it would be rash to determine which of these had been composed during his residence in the asylum, although some of them undoubtedly were. One of these (Nov. 1844), beginning 'The harp so loved awakes no more,' bears internal evidence of mental gloom, and may be claimed as belonging to this period, although it was sent to the editor long subsequently to Mr Riddell's discharge. In addition to the medical and protective means of treatment adopted, and in addition to daily and prolonged conferences and confidences which were resorted to in order to enable the patient to lay bare the whole extent of his perplexity and distress, and to enable the physician to afford whatever consolation or support could be derived from presenting truthful and healthy impressions to his mind, and from exposing indirectly the errors into which he had fallen— repeated attempts were made to rouse him from the state of stolidity or passivity into which he fell, after the disappearance of specific delusions, by reference to his family, former position, and usefulness, by reading aloud portions of his own published poetry and of Border minstrelsy, &c., by inducing him to take exercise in the surrounding country, to join in appropriate amusements, and to stimulate the attention and powers of mind generally by the infliction of slight degrees of pain, by means of application of blisters, &c. At one time a marked approach to convalescence could be observed; he could be engaged in general conversation, and spoke clearly and consecutively; he appeared to have denuded himself of all delusions, and described his mind as prostrate before a sense of confusion and inexplicability, and a vague apprehension of coming evil. There is reason to believe that the original delusions never afterwards excited any influence over his mind, and that his look and expression of pain, difficulty, and dread proceeded from his inability to comprehend the new position into which he had been thrown, and to struggle against the misfortunes which his consciousness of his impairment of power seemed to portend. His friends imagining that his removal to new scenes, and the consequent necessity for self-exertion and self-control, might call forth what faculties remained, he returned home. The restoration was not, however, complete. There are indeed grounds for believing that he again sunk into profound melancholy, during which, although living in silence and seclusion, and apart from his family, he felt constrained, by the mastery of a spirit which seemed at variance to his own, or external to his consciousness, to engage in composition, and actually produced enormous numbers of verses of various degrees of excellence, a metrical translation of the Psalms, &c. In a letter in my possession, he describes the little closet in which he was accustomed to immure himself, surrounded knee-deep by MSS., and where he conceived he was compelled to undergo a sort of penance or doom, and from which he could not escape. The friendship thus commenced between us, on his part in the struggle to obtain comfort and support, and on mine in sympathy and in the sincere desire to afford relief, has never ceased nor waned. After he had entirely regained his former health and serenity, he commenced a correspondence with me, dictated by a wish to obtain my opinion as to doubts which then disturbed him as to the propriety of resuming his ministerial, and especially his pulpit, duties. This was followed by placing at my disposal various unpublished poems, written, as it was understood, both while in the asylum, immediately after his return to Carnlanrig, and at other times, for insertion in the periodical which had commenced, and was conducted by patients, and which still continues. Subsequently to this, but I cannot say in what year, he paid a visit to Dumfriesshire, when he introduced to me his son William, a boy of brilliant abilities and extraordinary promise; and I can recollect very vividly the pride and affection and fancy with which he sketched out the future of his gifted representative—a future, alas! never to be realised."

After his recovery, which was complete and permanent, Mr Riddell did not again resume his ministerial duties. His autobiography, which was written in 1854, he concludes thus: "'The Christian Politician'* was published during the time of my indisposition. This work I had written at leisure hours, with the hopes of its being beneficial to the people placed under my care, by giving them a general and connected view of the principles and philosophical bearing of the Christian religion. In exhorting them privately, I discovered that many of them understood that religion better in itself than they appeared to comprehend the manner in which it stood in connection with the surrounding circumstances of this life. In other words, they were acquainted with doctrines and principles whose application and use, whether in regard to thought, or feeling, or daily practice, they did not so clearly recognise. To remedy this state of things I wrote 'The Christian Politician' in a style as simple as the subjects treated of in it would well admit of, giving it a conversational cast, instead of systematic

* "The Christian Politician, or the Right Way of Thinking." Edinburgh, 1844, 8vo.

arrangement, that it might be the less forbidding to those for whom it was principally intended. Being published, however, at the time when, through my indisposition, I could take no interest in it, it was sent forth in a somewhat more costly shape than rightly suited the original design; and although extensively introduced and well received, it was in society of a higher order than that which it was its object chiefly to benefit.

"My latest publication is a volume of 'Poems and Songs,'* published by Messrs Sutherland and Knox of Edinburgh. 'The Cottagers of Glendale,' the 'Lay of Life,' and some others of the compositions in this volume, were written during the period of my convalescence; the songs are, for the greater part, the production of 'the days of other years.' Many of the latter had been already sung in every district of the kingdom, but had been much corrupted in the course of oral transmission. These wanderers of the hill-harp are now secured in a permanent form."

The narrative of the remaining part of Mr Riddell's life may be briefly told. By the generosity of the Duke of Buccleuch he was allowed to retain the cottage that was erected for him when minister of the charge of Teviothead, and a parcel of land around it;

* "Poems, Songs, and Miscellaneous Pieces." Edinburgh 1847, 12mo.

and from the same source he also enjoyed a small annual grant of money. He took no prominent part in any of the great movements of the day, and for a man of his acknowledged ability may be said to have led the life of a recluse. Almost the only sign the outside world, and this only a part of the south of Scotland, had of his existence, was the occasional appearance of his name in the Poets' Corner of some local newspaper, or his rare appearance on the platform of one of the neighbouring towns as a lecturer. So much was this the case, that when the death of the author of "Scotland yet" was announced through the whole press of the country, many of those best versed in our national literature were astonished that he had been living up till that time. But although spent in this manner, his life was happy beyond the lot of most men. Several circumstances contributed to this, but perhaps the most important was his singularly contented disposition. Few can treat the cares and annoyances of this world with the same equanimity. He never looked for causes of offences, and consequently seldom found them; but when they came unmistakably, as he himself never wilfully gave offence, he was able to look upon them with pity instead of anger. Another source of happiness was—the somewhat unusual one for a poet—want of ambition. What the world thought of his productions, whether his name would descend to posterity occupying an honoured place among the poets of his native land, or be shortly forgotten, never apparently cost him a thought; and if it did, it was not a matter of solicitude. This was unfortunate in one respect, for it has hitherto deprived us of the pleasure of becoming familiar with some of his best compositions. Another source, and certainly not the least productive, was his own fireside. In Mrs Riddell, who still survives, his first and only love, the Eliza of his songs, he had experience of all the virtues that a wife can possibly possess. She was the daughter of Mr William Clark, a merchant in Biggar. Their early attachment, and subsequent union, are mentioned in terms of great affection in his autobiography. But their wedded life was not without its trials. Of these the greatest was Mr Riddell's indisposition, already fully alluded to. Another great affliction was the death of their second son William, who died at the early age of twenty. He was a young man of great promise, had great facileness in acquiring knowledge, was learned in many languages, and had given undoubted proofs of being possessed of true poetical genius. Of their two remaining sons, Walter, the eldest, is in the employment of the Hong-Kong and Shanghai Bank; and the other, Robert, is engaged in farming pursuits in Australia. In his means Mr Riddell was peculiarly fortunate. What Agur prayed for was granted to him. He had " neither poverty nor riches." For money he cared nothing ; but at the same time he had a great horror of debt, and studiously avoided it.

He was never idle. It was his usual custom to rise with the sun, and retire to rest at an early hour, unless when prompted by some irresistible inspiration of the muse, which rendered sleep impossible. This, however, seldom occurred, for she was more his servant than he was hers. His mind was well in hand, and as a rule it only became possessed when allowed to do so. A large amount of his time was occupied in looking after the interests of his little holding. Although his acreage was small, it was large enough to entail a considerable amount of labour, and at the same time gratify his inclination for farming. But when engaged in these pursuits his mind was seldom wholly taken up with them. Indeed, he often averred that he could compose best when he had a hoe, a spade, a rake, or a scythe in his hands ; for ideas came most freely when least sought after. His work as a farmer was not mere routine. He continually carried on a system of improvement. When he assumed possession of the place, it was anything but inviting. Most of the land was little better than a marsh. The house was situated on the verge of a morass, and

was flanked on either side by a mountain torrent,
neither of which had any particular limits. In fact,
they often joined company, and left no other means
of proving their individual identity than the bard's
house standing up as a landmark between them. It
may seem strange that such an unforbidding locality
should ever have been chosen for the site of a human
residence, but the reason is not far to seek. Con-
tending interests on the part of adjoining tenants of
the Buccleuch estate left the superior no choice.
Nature in this, as often in affairs of greater magni-
tude, wrought its own cure. The stream on the
west, by deepening its bed, enabled him to drain off
the waters of the marsh, and thus also it was prevented from overflowing its banks ; while the same
object was attained on the east by diverting the
brook from its original course to a considerable distance from the house. In this manner the land was
improved, and the house placed beyond water-mark.
These circumstances have been particularly mentioned, because to Mr Riddell it was a scene of
labour and interest for years. During all that time,
and indeed to the end of his life, he was occupied
in adding to the beauty of his home. This he did,
not by making artistic squares and circles with plants
in an unnatural state of existence, but by imitating
the arrangements of nature. Thus we find the place
presents little regularity, and the trees which adorn

and shelter it are mostly Scotch fir, hawthorn, birch, alder, willow, or others indigenous to the district. A different arrangement obtained with regard to his shrubs and flowers. These he selected on a different principle. They were mementoes of friendly places and people. There is not a plant amongst them but has its own history and associations. Most of them were brought from Stobo, Posso, and other localities in Tweedside as well as Clydesdale, where they were culled and carefully preserved during his annual visits to these districts. In this manner, truly it may be said that he created the place; for without other aid than his own hands, that lovely spot, which now bears so striking a record of his taste and industry, has been gradually emerged from one of the most dismal swamps in Teviotdale.

But although the site of his dwelling originally was miserable in its minute details, the locality is undoubtedly one of the best that could have been selected for a pastoral poet's dwelling. It may be called the land of his nativity, for Teviothead Cottage, where he lived so long, and where he died, is not more than seven miles from Sorbie, where he was born. His different residences lay within narrow bounds— an area of ten miles compasses them all. But within that limit is included one of the richest and most beautiful districts of all that is rich and beautiful in pastoral Scotland. The green hills of Teviotdale, on whose swards the plough has not yet intruded, and over which the sheep and its shepherd still reign supreme, yield in nothing to the much-lauded and often-sung, and consequently classic, regions of Ettrick and Yarrow. It was his own land, and its inhabitants were his "ain folk." Most of them are engaged in farming pursuits, and a more quiet, contented, warm-hearted, intelligent rural population is not to be found anywhere. They reverenced him as their poet; and to show how great was their reverence, ten years ago they presented him with a " guid auld harp." They loved him as their friend; and the love was mutual. The locality, as stated, is one of great natural beauty. Before the vale of the Teviot terminates by breaking up into a number of narrow glens, which it does about half a mile further up, it expands into a sort of amphitheatre, and in the very centre of this stands the poet's house, embosomed in a small clump of trees, the most prominent object in the landscape. In front of it runs the Teviot, and flowing down to mingle their waters with the parent river on either side descends a mountain stream; while not more than a gunshot to the north lies a richly-wooded glen, with its rocks and waterfalls and old British fort. To the end of his life this was his favourite resort, and here many of his best songs were composed. It is the "wild glen sae green," where

" Adown the burn beneath the shaw,
   There grows a bonnie birken tree,
That waves aboon the water-fa'
   Whene'er the breeze comes o'er the lea."

But the district has other attractions than the worth of its inhabitants and the beauty of its scenery. It is part of the land of Border feud and foray, and many traditions relating to these lawless times still linger among its glens. Several of the places mentioned in the exquisite ballad of " Jamie Telfer of the fair Dodhead " are in Teviothead, and Jamie's kye must have been driven th ugh the whole length of the parish, for

" The gear was driven the Frostylee up,
   Frae Frostylee unto the plain."

Perhaps its most interesting association is connected with the fate of the renowned freebooter, Johnie Armstrong of Gilnockie. At Carlenrig chapel, where Teviothead parish church now stands, he and thirty-six of his retainers were hanged by King James V. in 1529. The king had undertaken an expedition to impose law on the lawless borderers. Unaware of the fate of Cockburn of Henderland and Scott of Tushielaw, Johnie, with full faith in the royal clemency and with a due appreciation of his own services to his country, presented himself before his sovereign unarmed, and arrayed in all the barbaric splendour of the time. Pitscottie describes the interview thus: "James, looking upon him sternly, said to his attendants, 'What wants that knave that a king should have?' and ordered him and his followers to instant execution. But Johnie made great offers to the king. That he should sustain himself with forty gentlemen, ever ready at his service, on their own cost, without wronging any Scottishman; secondly, that there was not a subject in England, duke, earl, or baron, but within a certain day he should bring him to his majesty either quick or dead. At length, he, seeing no hope of favour, said very proudly, 'It is folly to seek grace at a graceless face; but,' said he, 'had I known this, I should have lived upon the Borders in despite of King Henry and you both; for I know King Henry would downweigh my best horse with gold to know that I were condemned to die this day.'" The result was, as is well known,

> " John murdered was at Carlinrigg,
>   And all his gallant companie;
> But Scotland's heart was ne'er sae wae,
>   To see sae mony brave men die."

With all these traditions Mr Riddell was well acquainted and greatly interested, and no doubt they served largely to increase his attachment to the district. Often has the writer of this heard him tell the tale of Johnie Armstrong and his " gallant companie," and in doing so his heart seemed to be, like

that of Scotland, " ne'er sae wae." He had great
faith in kings and their prerogatives—was in fact a
good old Tory—but he could never justify King James
for his cruel act, which he always characterised as a
breach of trust, and something very like treachery.
His loyalty was great, but his patriotism was greater.

There are traditions, too, of later date, but scarcely
less interesting, relating to Prince Charles Edward's
invasion of England; and in the same churchyard
where repose the mortal remains of the freebooter
and the poet also lie those of William Fraser, a fol-
lower of the Prince. This same Fraser seems to
have had discretion enough to see that a life, however menial, spent amidst the quietude of Teviothead, was preferable to the hardships and uncertain-
ties incident to following his natural chief. And
that he took kindly to the land of the Sassenach, like
many other of his countrymen, is evident, seeing
that he lived to the patriarchal age of 105. William
was very provident, and the stone which marks his
place of rest was secured by himself from the neighbouring Back-water.

Besides these objects of interest, the district is
rich in remains of its primitive inhabitants, of which
tradition does not even presume to tell the story.
On almost every hill-top there are the outlines of a
British strength; there are several sepulchral cairns
standing intact; and not more than two miles east

from the poet's dwelling there runs across the country the Catrail, that mysterious barrier or pathway, whose nature has formed a pregnant theme of speculation to antiquaries for more than a hundred years.

When not engaged with his farm he was either writing or reading. As a reader, he may be said to have been omnivorous—whatever came in his way he read. Although not mingling with the world, he took a keen interest in all that was being transacted in it, and never, if possible, missed his daily newspaper. If he was not at the post-office awaiting the arrival of the post-gig, you might rest assured that some strong tie prevented him. As in duty bound, he was thoroughly conversant with all the poetry in our literature, ancient and modern, and was critically acquainted with the writings of all those who are entitled to be called standard novelists. The novels of Sir Walter Scott, with the exception of the dramatic works of Shakespeare, he looked upon as the greatest literary products of human genius. History, however, was the favourite subject of his reading ; and in it, with the exception of dates, he was extremely well versed. Dates were his bugbear. He could tell the order of sequence in which any given events occurred, but he could seldom state the year. At the time of his death he was engaged reading, for the second or third time,

Alison's 'History of Europe' and Tytler's 'History of Scotland.'

His writing for many years back has consisted principally in copying his earlier productions, and in composing tales relating to Border chivalry. His copying - work had a twofold object. The mere exercise of writing, at least when writing his own compositions, gave him great pleasure, and he had a belief that at some future period, when he could give no assistance, his works would be called for by the public ; so he tried to put them into proper form for the printer. Owing to their great length, some of them would form a goodly volume of themselves: only two of these Tales will appear in the present edition of his works. To say anything more of those which are kept back, than that they are full of incident and interest, would be out of place, as it is likely they will soon all be presented to the public. During the same time he also composed many songs, and several poems bearing on current events, most of which appeared in the local newspapers of the day. Some of these are embraced in the present publication. In 1847 Mr Riddell contributed a biographical sketch of James Hogg, the Ettrick Shepherd, to 'Hogg's Instructor.' It extended through three numbers of the journal, and gives a most faithful and interesting account of his mental peculiarities, and of all the leading incidents of his life. In 1855 he translated the Gospel of St Matthew, and in 1857 the Psalms, into Lowland Scotch, for Prince Louis Lucien Bonaparte. As this was accomplished in connection with the private studies of that distinguished philologist, they were not published, and only a very limited number of them was printed. From Mr Riddell's intimate acquaintance with the peculiar terms and phraseology of his native district, the selection of him as translator was most fortunate. Some of his renderings are extremely happy; and if imperfections and mistakes can be pointed out, the difficulty of the task, as well as that his was the first attempt to render the Scriptures into the Scotch language, must be borne in mind. For years back he had devoted much time and labour to producing a reply to the Colenso heresies, and had amassed a large amount of manuscript on the subject. But the undertaking was a mistake, and was reluctantly abandoned. His reading on the topic was insufficient, and a library containing the books necessary for reference was not within his reach. But perhaps his greatest deficiency lay in the want of sufficient scholarship, for, as he tells us in his autobiography, he was not " proficient in mathematical lore." Besides the productions mentioned, he wrote a number of tales in prose, of a similar nature to Wilson's 'Tales of the Borders.' None of these have been published.

It may well be wondered why a man of his undoubted ability should not have taken a prominent part in the periodical literature of his day. This is easily explained. His nature was not obtrusive. Unless a thing was forced upon him, he never thought of it; and instead of a deficiency, the magazines have a plethora of writers.

It has been casually mentioned that he sometimes lectured in the neighbouring towns. This was generally done for some charitable object, and he never appeared as a paid lecturer. His most frequent subjects were in connection with Border literature. As a lecturer he was always popular, although he never had, nor assumed to have, the gift of eloquence. Nevertheless, his strong full voice and distinct pronunciation, the frequent interspersions of his native Doric, his striking appearance and acknowledged position as a poet, taken in connection with the never-to-be-mistaken fulness of his knowledge of whatever subject he took in hand, always assured for him a success that many more pretentious lecturers might well have been proud of.

For many years back, in company with Mrs Riddell, he made an annual visit to upper Tweeddale and Clydesdale. In these districts they had many friends, and in the neighbourhood of Biggar nearly all Mrs Riddell's relatives live. There they first met, and the pleasant associations of the days of their courtship were connected with it. No wonder, then, that he looked forward to this excursion with all the ardour of a schoolboy to his annual school vacation. But there were other circumstances which rendered it particularly enjoyable. In Clydesdale he was not in his own country, and was honoured accordingly. At Teviothead his presence might be counted on at any time; and although even there he was universally respected, he received comparatively little attention, seeing that it could be paid whenever inclination prompted. At Biggar it was different, for he was never there long enough to render himself familiar and commonplace. He was always the poet and the man of letters—one different from, and superior to, the common herd. This feeling was not diminished by the appearances in the pulpit and on the platform which he frequently made. Four years ago, in company with his relative the late Mr Jackson of Altarstone, the journey was prolonged into the West Highlands. But although the solemn beauty of the lakes, the rich scenery of the glens, and the rugged magnificence of the mountains impressed him greatly, and, as he said, " filled his whole soul with adoration and wonderment," yet nothing came of it. He admired them like any other tourist possessed of a keen appreciation of the beautiful and sublime, but his muse was silent.

Why was this? Could she only drink inspiration from the quiet pastoral scenes of her native Borderland? Had she attained her full stature, and lost all the plasticity of youth?

Born a shepherd's son, and reared a shepherd himself, he naturally took a keen interest in, and was intimately acquainted with, all the details of sheep-farming. Indeed, his knowledge in this department of farming far exceeded that of most men who have made it their life-long pursuit and study. In 1848 and 1849 he published in the 'Scottish Agricultural Journal' a series of papers on "Store-Farming in the South of Scotland," which those best able to judge pronounce very valuable. In these he gives an interesting account of the introduction of the breed of Cheviot sheep into the country, and of the state in which the country was at the time of their introduction. They contain many valuable hints on the improvement of pasture-lands and the management of stock, especially during the winter season. About the same time he sent to the Highland and Agricultural Society an "Essay on Foot-Rot in Sheep," for which he was awarded a prize of ten pounds.

That love of antiquities, which we find first manifesting itself in making explorations in the deserted churchyard of Buccleuch when he was a mere boy, continued through life. In 1869 he formed one of a party who made several interesting excursions and excavations in Teviothead. One of these took place at Teindside, and brought to light several valuable remains of the early inhabitants of the district. This he has celebrated in "The Grave of the Unknown." About the same time he also superintended the removal of two sepulchral cairns in the immediate neighbourhood of his own dwelling. But these yielded only some calcined bones and an iron spear-head. In the article "Cavers" which he contributed to Sir John Sinclair's 'Statistical Account of Scotland,' all the most important objects of antiquity in that parish are described. He took great interest in the welfare of the Hawick Archæological Society, to which he contributed several papers. At the time of his death he was under promise to read another, in verse, on ancient Border chivalry. As an antiquary he was more conversant with, and took greater interest in, subjects relating to historic than prehistoric times.

His personal appearance was striking, and a stranger meeting him for the first time could not fail at once to perceive that he was in the presence of no ordinary man. Undoubtedly the possession of poetic genius in many instances manifests itself in some peculiarity or other, more easily perceived than described. That this was the case with Mr Riddell, the following incident would seem to show. While on a visit to Dumfries, during the lifetime of

Burns's widow, he was introduced to her by their
mutual friend, Mr M'Diarmid, the accomplished
editor of the 'Dumfries Courier.' Mrs Burns, being either unacquainted with the reputation of her
visitor, or not catching his name, and being, no
doubt, much annoyed with sight-seers, was at first
uncommunicative and reserved in her manner.
Gradually, however, as they got into conversation,
her reserve wore off, and her heart warmed. She
told him much about the poet, and showed many
relics of him which she still retained. When leaving, grasping his hand, she observed that of all the
men she had met, he bore the strongest resemblance
to her husband. But whether this referred to manner, style of conversation, or personal appearance,
there is no means of determining. In stature he
was somewhat above the average height, but a
slight stoop rendered this little apparent. His
shoulders were broad, his limbs large and brawny,
and his gait, although a little slouching, had a
springy firmness in its step. His general outline
was rough and angular, and the most forcible impression it conveyed was the possession of rugged
muscular strength. His head was large, and the
hair flowed around it in long hoary weird locks.
His features were irregular, and, as he said of those
of his friend Hogg, beyond the powers of art to por-
tray. The portrait, however, which illustrates the

present volume, after a photograph by Horsburgh of Edinburgh, taken at the Melrose meeting of the Border Association in 1867, when he was sixty-nine years of age, is, nevertheless, an excellent likeness. A broad forehead, receding above, prominent below, fringed with long shaggy eyebrows, overhung keen grey eyes, always gleaming with kindliness, often showing a dash of wildness and satire, and which no one could ever catch without feeling that in them a warm heart found expression. His manner was plain and unassuming, but without any trace of vulgarity. He was a most pleasing companion, had an unlimited fund of information, and said clever things in a natural unstudied way. At home he was most hospitable, and delighted to see his friends, whom he spared no trouble to make comfortable and happy. Although he enjoyed society much, he was of a retiring disposition, and never went to any place unless specially invited. As it was only from his writings that a proper idea of his mental powers and peculiarities could be obtained, these have not, in justice both to the poet and his readers, been attempted to be analysed.

His connection with the Border Counties Association has been left to the end of this notice because of the sad relation its last annual meeting had to his death. The history of the association is briefly this. In 1865 a number of gentlemen belonging to the south of Scotland, resident in Edinburgh, determined to form a Border society, embracing the counties of Roxburgh, Berwick, and Selkirk, having for its object the encouragement of friendly intercourse among its members, and the promotion of education in the district embraced. The subject had often been mooted before; but although several similar societies were already in existence, it had always fallen to the ground. Now, however, it proved a great success, and this has to be attributed in a great measure to the unwearied exertion and true Border spirit of Mr Thomas Usher. In 1866 Mr Riddell was elected an honorary member, and to the end of his life took a great interest in its prosperity. He was present at three of its meetings—at one annual meeting in Edinburgh, and at the local meetings at Melrose and Selkirk—and at all of them he acted a prominent part. For the Melrose meeting he composed 'Our fair Borderland,' and at Selkirk he proposed the memory of Sir Walter Scott in an able and effective speech. In him the members found a man according to their own hearts—one who formed a connecting-link between the present and the times that had passed away; who not only knew everything relating to the present state of the Borders, but had also a mind well stored with all its old-world lore. He was their "last minstrel," and his songs formed their staple music; consequently his receptions were most cordial. It was a pleasant sight to see the old man listening with apparent delight to his own songs, sung amid the applause of his fellow-Borderers. The last local meeting of the Association took place at Hawick on the 28th of July 1870. A toast had been assigned to Mr Riddell, but he did not appear at the dinner, and many were the conjectures as to the cause of his absence. A dinner of the Association at Hawick without him was like a feast without the host—he was the greatest member of the district. But the explanation soon came, and in a way little anticipated. Its purport is conveyed in the following letter to Mr Usher, the secretary :—

" TEVIOTHEAD COTTAGE, *July* 28, 1870.

" MY DEAR SIR,—My wife's ill health, together with my own, prevents me from being at your meeting to-day. After much pain and toil through the night, I rose this morning still resolved to be with you, and to reply to the toast the best I could which you did me the honour of assigning to me ; but, instead of taking the road, I found that I had enough ado to get to the sofa. I am sad of soul and heart through serious concerns of mind, as well as bodily indisposition. I have taken some medicine, and hope to be in better trim ere very long, though I can for the present scarcely scribble this apology. I plead with you to accept of it yourself, and make the best use of it in regard to others that you possibly can. My intention was to be down and remain in Hawick, as you requested, that I might have the pleasure of conversing with you in private ; but 'the best laid schemes o' mice and men gang aft agly,' and this is all up for the present. You mention some request to be made, which, you may rest assured, will be heartily complied with to the very utmost of my power.

"I hope you will let me hear from you. If my wife can manage to travel by any means, she intends to go to the seaside, and I along with her, God willing. I shall then have the pleasure of seeing you. . . .

"Excuse this miserable scrawling ; and may Heaven now and evermore bless thee and thine.—I am, my dear sir, yours very truly, HENRY SCOTT RIDDELL."

Before the meeting was over, the writer of this biography was summoned to see him, and on going to Teviothead found him suffering from one of the most painful and hopeless maladies incident to the human frame. Unchecked by remedies, the disease ran its course, and after six-and-thirty hours of intense suffering, borne with Christian resignation and patience, the gentle spirit of the good old man returned to God who gave it. On the 2d of August, surrounded by a great concourse of friends and admirers from far and near, all that was mortal of the Bard of Teviotdale was laid in its last resting-place, in that

" Churchyard that lonely is lying
Amid the deep greenwood by Teviot's wild strand."

www.ingramcontent.com/pod-product-compliance
Lightning Source LLC
Chambersburg PA
CBHW081521040426
42447CB00013B/3297